Primary Sources in World History

THE RENAISSANCE

ENZO GEORGE

Cavendish Square
New York

Published in 2017 by Cavendish Square Publishing, LLC
243 5th Avenue, Suite 136 New York, NY 10016

© 2017 Brown Bear Books Ltd

Website: cavendishsq.com

This publication represents the opinions and views of the author based on his or her personal experiences, knowledge, and research. The information in this book serves as a general guide only. The author and publisher have used their best efforts in preparing this book and disclaim liabilty rising directly or indirectly for the use and application of this book.

CPSIA compliance information: Batch #CS16CSQ.

All websites were available and accurate when this book went to press.

Library of Congress Cataloging-in-Publication Data

Names: George, Enzo.
Title: The Renaissance / Enzo George.
Description: New York : Cavendish Square, 2016. | Series: Primary sources in world history | Includes index.
Identifiers: ISBN 9781502618092 (library bound) | ISBN 9781502618115 (ebook)
Subjects: LCSH: Renaissance—Juvenile literature. | Europe—History—476-1492—Juvenile literature.
Classification: LCC D117.G46 2016 | DDC 940.2'1—dc23

For Brown Bear Books Ltd:
Editorial Director: Lindsey Lowe
Managing Editor: Tim Cooke
Children's Publisher: Anne O'Daly
Design Manager: Keith Davis
Designer: Lynne Lennon
Picture Manager: Sophie Mortimer

Picture Credits:
Front Cover: Getty Images: DEA/Veneranda Biblioteca Ambrosiana main; Shutterstock: ilolab map.
Interior: Biblioteca Ambrosiana: 8; Biblioteca Nacional de Espana: 6; Convent of Santa Maria della Grazie: 16; Dreamstime: Izanbar 31; Frick Collection: 36; Galleria dagli Uffizi 13, 17; Geraki: 10; Kunsthistorisches Museum, Vienna: 39; L'Histoire: 42; Louvre Museum, Paris: 18; Museo Firenze com'era: 22; National Gallery: 37; Royal Picture Gallery Mauritshuis: 25; Shutterstock: Frank Bach 40, Chris Dorney 33, Edella 34, Shanna Hyatt 24, Anton Ivanov 26, Timur Kulgarin 14, LianeM 12, Vlacheslav Lopatin 7, Marco Saracco 27, Renata Sedmakova 32, SJ Travel Photo & Video 15, Takespicsforfun 11, Thinkstock: Janka Dharmasena 19, Icharis 77 28, B.P. Perry ifc, 9, Photos.com 20, Floriano Rescigno 38; Topfoto: Fine Art Images/Heritage Images 41, 43, Ullstein bild 23, World History Archive 21: York Project: Accademia Carrara 30, Santa Maria Gloriosa dei Frari 29, Uffizi Gallery 35.

Brown Bear Books has made every attempt to contact the copyright holder.
If you have any information please contact licensing@brownbearbooks.co.uk

We believe the extracts included in this book to be material in the public domain.
Anyone having further information should contact licensing@brownbearbooks.co.uk

All rights reserved. No part of this book may be reproduced, stored in a retrieval system, or transmitted in any form or by any means, electronic, mechanical, photocopying, recording, or otherwise, without the prior written permission of the copyright holder.

Printed in the United States of America

CONTENTS

Introduction 4
A Rebirth of Knowledge 6
The Divine Comedy 8
Fall of Constantinople 10
City-States in Italy 12
Florence Under the Medici 14
Developments in Art 16
Leonardo Da Vinci 18
The Growth of Trade 20
The Rise of Banking 22
Towns and Wealth 24
Architecture 26
Renaissance Venice 28
Politics and Government 30
The Catholic Church 32
The Papacy 34
Humanism 36
Northern Renaissance 38
Tudor England 40
The Sack of Rome 42
Timeline 44
Glossary 46
Further Information 47
Index 48

INTRODUCTION

Primary sources are the best way to get close to people from the past. They include the things people wrote in diaries, letters, or books; the paintings, drawings, maps, or cartoons they created; and even the buildings they constructed, the clothes they wore, or the objects they owned. Such sources often reveal a lot about how people saw themselves and how they thought about their world.

This book collects a range of primary sources from the Renaissance, a period in European history that followed on from the Middle Ages. As rough markers of its start and end, some historians date the Renaissance period as lasting from about 1300 to about 1550.

Many Europeans who lived in the Renaissance believed that they were creating a new world. They studied books and art from ancient Greece and Rome. European thinkers used these classical works as the basis of a philosophy called humanism, which placed the experience of individuals and reason above supernatural concerns. The word renaissance means "rebirth"—people thought they were bringing classical ideas back to life. The new way of thinking spread quickly throughout the rich cities of Italy and northern Europe. Eventually it would influence art, literature, and politics—virtually all aspects of European life.

THE RENAISSANCE

HOW TO USE THIS BOOK

Each spread contains at least one primary source. Look out for "Source Explored" boxes that explain images from the Renaissance and who made them and why. There are also "As They Saw It" boxes that contain quotes from people of the period.

Some boxes contain more detailed information about a particular aspect of a subject. The subjects are arranged in roughly chronological order. They focus on key events or people. There is a full timeline of the period at the back of the book.

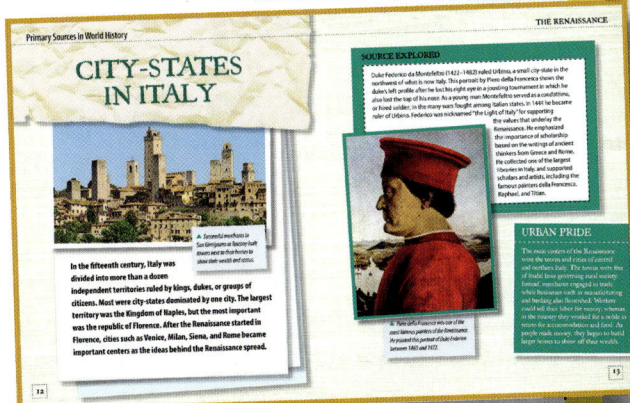

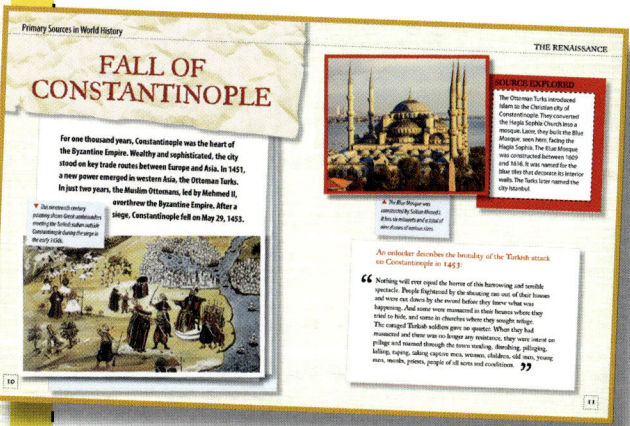

Some spreads feature a longer extract from a contemporary eyewitness. Look for the colored introduction that explains who the writer is and the origin of his or her account. These accounts are often accompanied by a related visual primary source.

5

Primary Sources in World History

A REBIRTH OF KNOWLEDGE

▲ This illustration entitled The Triumph of Love *comes from a collection of poems written in the 1340s by the Renaissance poet and scholar Petrarch.*

The word Renaissance is French for "rebirth." Scholars in the Renaissance period began to revive the ideas of the thinkers of ancient Greece and Rome. A key influence was the rediscovery of texts by philosophers such as Plato and Aristotle. Many texts had been preserved by Muslim scholars in the Middle East. They were now translated into Latin. These texts encouraged thinkers and artists to value the experience of the individual over ideas that were based on religious teaching. With the invention of the printing press in Germany around 1440 books were easier to make and new ideas spread quickly.

THE RENAISSANCE

◀ *The School of Athens was one of three frescoes Raphael painted in the same room in the papal apartments. This fresco celebrated philosophy: the other two celebrated theology and literature.*

SOURCE EXPLORED

The Florentine painter Raphael painted a series of frescoes in the papal apartments in the Vatican for Pope Julius II. This fresco, *The School of Athens*, was completed from 1508 to 1511. The fresco shows famous philosophers from Greece and Rome in an idealized setting. At its center walk the two most influential ancient thinkers: Plato (*in red*) and his student, Artistotle (*in blue*). The painting reveals how important classical thinking was in the Renaissance. It was painted for the head of the Catholic Church yet showed philosophers from a time before the birth of Christianity. Renaissance thinkers believed the ancients had discussed Christian ideas without being aware of it, and that their ideas could be applied to Christian beliefs.

AS THEY SAW IT

" It is but in our own day that men dare boast that they see the dawn of better things.... Now indeed, may every thoughtful spirit thank God that he has been permitted to be born in this new age, so full of hope and promise, which already rejoices in a greater array of nobly gifted souls than the world has seen in the thousand years which preceded it. "

—Matteo Palmieri, a Florentine thinker, writes about the Renaissance in *On Civic Life* (written in 1429, printed in 1528).

Primary Sources in World History

THE DIVINE COMEDY

Italians call the Florentine poet Dante Alighieri the father of the Italian language. When he wrote his epic poem, *The Divine Comedy* (circa 1308–1320), he wrote it in Italian rather than Latin, which was then seen as the language of poetry. By writing in Italian, Dante made his work accessible to people who had not been educated in Latin. His decision influenced contemporary writers such as Petrarch and Boccaccio. Dante's description of a journey through Hell, Purgatory, and Heaven was one of the earliest expressions of the humanist thinking of the Renaissance.

◀ This illustration comes from a Renaissance copy of the poems of the Roman poet Virgil (first century BCE). Renaissance writers drew on classical examples in their works.

THE RENAISSANCE

◀ To the right of Dante in this picture is the dome of Florence cathedral. To the left is Hell, through which the poet travels in The Divine Comedy. Behind Dante is the Mount of Purgatory with Adam and Eve on the top, indicating an earthly paradise.

SOURCE EXPLORED

The artist Domenico de Michelino painted this fresco of Dante in Florence Cathedral in 1465. By then the poet had been dead for over a century, but the fresco reflects his reputation. Dante holds a copy of *The Divine Comedy* as he stands between Florence (*right*) and the imagined world of his poem. In real life, the poet was exiled from Florence as a result of a bitter struggle between rival political groups. In Dante's poem, he is accompanied by the ancient Roman poet Virgil as he passes through Hell, where the souls of the wicked are punished. They visit Purgatory, where souls wait to be purified to enter Heaven, and finally enter Heaven itself. Dante used his poem to criticize the way he had been exiled by his fellow citizens of Florence.

AS THEY SAW IT

" Dante was the first to open the way for the return of the Muses banished from Italy. It was he who revealed the glory of the Florentine idiom. It was he who brought under the rule of due numbers every beauty of the vernacular [everyday] speech. It was he who may truly be said to have brought dead poetry back to life. "

—The writer Giovanni Boccaccio lectures about Dante in 1373.

Primary Sources in World History

FALL OF CONSTANTINOPLE

For one thousand years, Constantinople was the heart of the Byzantine Empire. Wealthy and sophisticated, the city stood on key trade routes between Europe and Asia. In 1451, a new power emerged in western Asia, the Ottoman Turks. In just two years, the Muslim Ottomans, led by Mehmed II, overthrew the Byzantine Empire. After a siege, Constantinople fell on May 29, 1453.

▼ This nineteenth century painting shows Greek ambassadors meeting the Turkish sultan outside Constantinople during the siege in the early 1450s.

THE RENAISSANCE

▲ The Blue Mosque was constructed by Sultan Ahmed I. It has six minarets and a total of nine domes of various sizes.

SOURCE EXPLORED

The Ottoman Turks introduced Islam to the Christian city of Constantinople. They converted the Hagia Sophia church into a mosque. Later, they built the Blue Mosque, seen here, facing the Hagia Sophia. The Blue Mosque was constructed between 1609 and 1616. It was named for the blue tiles that decorate its interior walls. The Turks later named the city Istanbul.

An onlooker describes the brutality of the Turkish attack on Constantinople in 1453:

" Nothing will ever equal the horror of this harrowing and terrible spectacle. People frightened by the shouting ran out of their houses and were cut down by the sword before they knew what was happening. And some were massacred in their houses where they tried to hide, and some in churches where they sought refuge. The enraged Turkish soldiers gave no quarter. When they had massacred and there was no longer any resistance, they were intent on pillage and roamed through the town stealing, disrobing, pillaging, killing, raping, taking captive men, women, children, old men, young men, monks, priests, people of all sorts and conditions. "

Primary Sources in World History

CITY-STATES IN ITALY

▲ *Successful merchants in San Gimignano in Tuscany built towers next to their homes to show their wealth and status.*

In the fifteenth century, Italy was divided into more than a dozen independent territories ruled by kings, dukes, or groups of citizens. Most were city-states dominated by one city. The largest territory was the Kingdom of Naples, but the most important was the republic of Florence. After the Renaissance started in Florence, cities such as Venice, Milan, Siena, and Rome became important centers as the ideas behind the Renaissance spread.

THE RENAISSANCE

SOURCE EXPLORED

Duke Federico da Montefeltro (1422–1482) ruled Urbino, a small city-state in the northwest of what is now Italy. This portrait by Piero della Francesca shows the duke's left profile after he lost his right eye in a jousting tournament in which he also lost the top of his nose. As a young man Montefeltro served as a *condottiero*, or hired soldier, in the many wars fought among Italian states. In 1444 he became ruler of Urbino. Federico was nicknamed "the Light of Italy" for supporting the values that underlay the Renaissance. He emphasized the importance of scholarship based on the writings of ancient thinkers from Greece and Rome. He collected one of the largest libraries in Italy, and supported scholars and artists, including the famous painters della Francesca, Raphael, and Titian.

▲ *Piero della Francesca was one of the most famous painters of the Renaissance. He painted this portrait of Duke Federico between 1465 and 1472.*

URBAN PRIDE

The main centers of the Renaissance were the towns and cities of central and northern Italy. The towns were free of feudal laws governing rural society. Instead, merchants engaged in trade, while businesses such as manufacturing and banking also flourished. Workers could sell their labor for money, whereas in the country they worked for a noble in return for accommodation and food. As people made money, they began to build larger homes to show off their wealth.

FLORENCE UNDER THE MEDICI

The Renaissance is usually said to have begun in Florence. The city was wealthy due to its wool trade and banking industry. In 1434, the banker Cosimo de Medici became the city's political leader. In 1532, the Medici became hereditary dukes. The family dominated Florence for over three hundred years. Four of them became popes. The Medici were supporters of the arts. Cosimo's grandson Lorenzo, who ruled Florence from 1469 to 1492, was nicknamed "the Magnificent" for his patronage of the arts.

◀ The prophet Abraham prepares to sacrifice his son in this bronze panel from 1401 by the sculptor Lorenzo Ghiberti. Ghiberti's panels decorated the doors of the Baptistery of San Giovanni in Florence. Michelangelo called one set of doors "the Gates of Paradise."

THE RENAISSANCE

◀ Florence is in the hills of Tuscany on the Arno River. The region was a center for silk and wool production during the Renaissance.

SOURCE EXPLORED

This view of Florence looks over the Arno River. The covered Ponte Vecchio ("Old Bridge") was built across the narrowest part of the river in 1345. In the distance is the dome of Florence's cathedral, designed by Filippo Brunelleschi and completed in 1436. By the fifteenth century, Florence was the largest city in Europe. Fortified walls protected its marketplaces and narrow streets, and the palaces of its leading families. Wealthy citizens and organizations provided work for artists, and Florence was at the forefront of all art forms. The city was developed as part of an ambitious project intended to portray it as an ideal city, which was a blend of order and beauty.

AS THEY SAW IT

" What city, not merely in Italy but in the whole world, is stronger within its walls, prouder in its palaces, richer in its temples, more lovely in its buildings ... Where is there trade richer in its variety? Where are there more famous men? "

—Coluccio Salutati, chancellor of Florence, praises the city in the late fourteenth century.

Primary Sources in World History

DEVELOPMENTS IN ART

▲ Leonardo da Vinci's The Last Supper *(circa 1495–1498)* was painted using new types of paint. However, his experiments meant the painting quickly started to decay.

Renaissance artists made many advances. They studied Greek and Roman art to learn about proportion. They studied the human body in order to create more realistic representations of the human form. Giotto di Bondone first introduced realistic figures to Christian art in the early fourteenth century. The subject matter of art also changed. Sandro Botticelli used ancient mythology rather than the Bible as the theme of his painting *The Birth of Venus* (c. 1484).

THE RENAISSANCE

SOURCE EXPLORED

The Battle of San Romano was painted by the Florentine artist Paolo Uccello in about 1438. It is an early example of linear perspective. This was a way to give an appearance of depth in a flat painting. The shapes of the horses show how Uccello tried to make them appear more solid. The broken lances lying on the ground are arranged to point toward an invisible vanishing point. Perspective was based on rules devised by the architect and engineer Filippo Brunelleschi in about 1413.

▲ Paolo Uccello's painting is one of three commemorating a victory for Florence over Siena in 1432.

The Florentine philosopher and priest Marsilio Ficino wrote to a friend in 1492 about the achievements of the Renaissance period in the arts and other fields:

" If we are to call any age golden, it is beyond doubt that age which brings forth golden talents in different places. That such is true of this our age [no one] will hardly doubt. For this century, like a golden age, has restored to light the liberal arts, which were almost extinct: grammar, poetry, rhetoric, painting, sculpture, architecture, music … and all this in Florence. Achieving what had been honored among the ancients, but almost forgotten since, the age has joined wisdom with eloquence, and prudence with the military art…. This century appears to have perfected astronomy. In Florence it has recalled the Platonic teaching from darkness into light … and in Germany … [there] have been invented the instruments for printing books. "

LEONARDO DA VINCI

The phrase "Renaissance Man" was invented to describe Leonardo da Vinci (1452–1519). It refers to someone who excels in a wide range of skills. Da Vinci was an outstanding painter, but he was also talented in military engineering, music, anatomy, botany, and literature. Leonardo worked for patrons in many Italian cities, including the Medici in Florence and Sforza family in Milan. Among his inventions were a flying machine and deadly weapons.

◀ *The Mona Lisa is* Leonardo's most famous painting—and probably the most famous painting in the world. It is said to be a portrait of a silk merchant's wife named Lisa Gherardini.

THE RENAISSANCE

SOURCE EXPLORED

These drawings from Leonardo's notebook show the muscles and tendons in a human arm. Between 1507 and 1513, Leonardo dissected more than thirty bodies and drew the most accurate anatomical studies then known. Leonardo used his knowledge of the mechanics of the body to paint more lifelike figures. Over his career, he filled 3,500 pages with sketches and ideas. He covered a wide range of subjects, but always used the same method. He closely observed something and then meticulously recorded it.

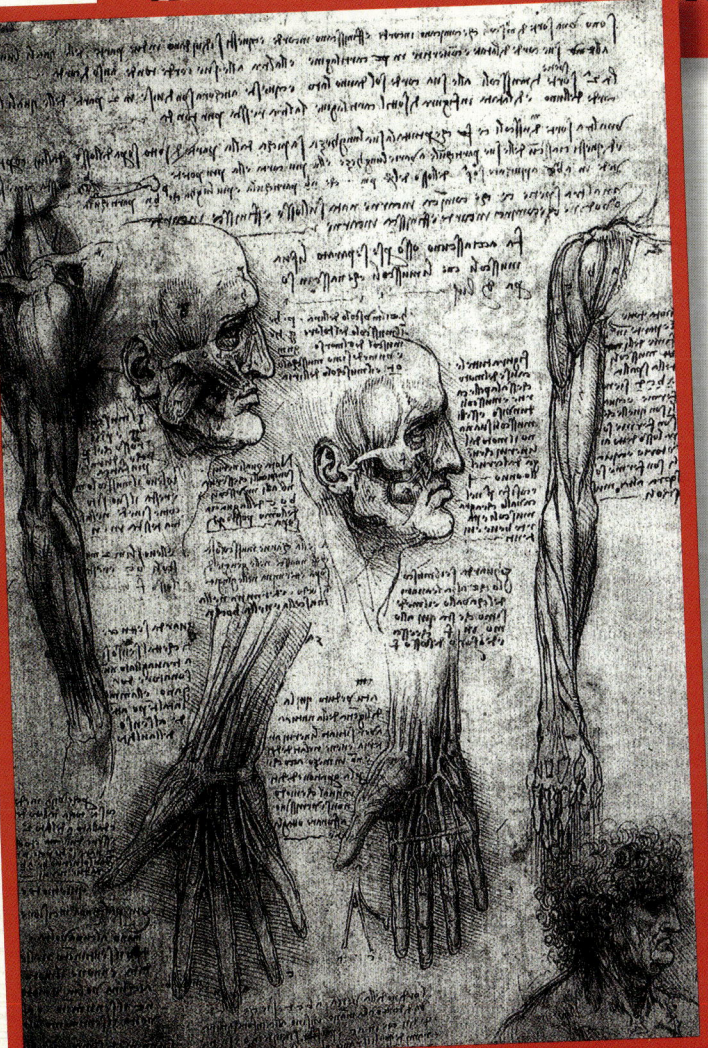

MONA LISA

The *Mona Lisa* is probably the most famous painting in the world. It may be a portrait of a merchant's wife named Lisa Gherardini. Leonardo began work on the portrait in about 1503 but continued to work on it for over fourteen years. He worked slowly, and only completed a few paintings in his career. *Mona Lisa* stands out for her mysterious half-smile and the way her eyes seem to look directly at the viewer.

◀ Leonardo used a mirror to write backwards in his notebooks so that no one else would be able to steal his ideas.

Primary Sources in World History

THE GROWTH OF TRADE

The Renaissance occurred partly because Italian rulers and merchants could afford to pay for artists and scholars. Italy's wealth came from trade between Europe in the west and Asia in the east. The ports of Venice and Genoa became rich and powerful from shipping, while in cities such as Florence families established banks that became very successful. While spices and ceramics from East Asia arrived in Italy via the Muslim Ottoman Empire, popular exports to Asia included woollen and silk fabrics that were woven in and around Florence.

◀ This painting from about 1400 shows the thirteenth-century merchant Marco Polo leaving Venice on a journey that took him to China.

THE RENAISSANCE

SOURCE EXPLORED

This painting from the fourteenth century shows men buying and selling goods in a covered market. The stalls include a shoemaker (*left*), a cloth merchant (*center*), and a man selling gold and silver (*right*). The Renaissance marked a break with medieval times. Previously, goods had usually been bartered, or exchanged for other goods. Now people made purchases with gold and silver coins. Each Italian city-state had its own coins, which were minted by the new banking houses. Coins were easier to transport and use than bars of silver and gold. That made it easier for merchants to trade with other merchants in distant places in Europe or throughout the Ottoman Empire. The gold florian of Florence was so widely traded it became the most important coin in Renaissance Europe.

AS THEY SAW IT

" Who could count the many shops so well furnished that they almost seem warehouses, with so many cloths of every make: tapestry, brocades and hangings of every design, carpets of every sort, camlets [sheets] of every color and texture, silks of every kind; and so many warehouses full of spices, groceries and drugs, and so much beautiful wax? These things stupefy the beholder. "

—Canon Pietro Casola reports on the goods that could be bought in Venice in the early sixteenth century.

▶ This miniature painting from the fourteenth century shows a marketplace. Trade increased throughout Europe in the early Renaissance.

21

Primary Sources in World History

THE RISE OF BANKING

In the Middle Ages, the Catholic Church said charging interest on a loan was a sin named usury. From the thirteenth century, however, thinkers argued that charging a fee for a loan did not count as usury. By the fourteenth century, banks started to lend money in return for a fee. The banks made huge fortunes—but they could also lose money if their loans were not repaid. The Peruzzi and Bardi families of Florence went bust when debtors, including the King of England, failed to pay their debts.

▶ The banking families of Florence used their wealth to build magnificent palaces. These Boboli Gardens were laid out by the wife of Cosimo Medici in 1550.

THE RENAISSANCE

▼ Jacob Fugger (right) talks to his chief accountant, Matthäus Schwarz, in the bank's counting house in Augsburg, Germany.

AS THEY SAW IT

"Here is the Rialto, which is a piazzetta [town square] … where business deals are made with a single word "yes" or "no." There are a large number of brokers, who are trustworthy… There are four banks… They hold very great amounts of money and issue credits under different names… Their decisions are binding."

—Marino Sanudo describes financial activity in the early sixteenth century in Venice.

SOURCE EXPLORED

This manuscript illustration shows the banker Jacob Fugger in his counting house in Augsburg, Germany, in 1517. The Fugger family made money from the textile and minerals trades before becoming some of Europe's most important bankers. Bankers in the Renaissance benefited from a number of practical advances. The first was the introduction in the mid-fourteenth century of letters of credit. A bank sent these letters on behalf of merchants to instruct another branch of the bank to pay money to a particular person. That enabled merchants to sell goods over long distances without having to transport gold or silver that could be stolen on the journey. The letters were like an early type of banknote. The second main advance was the invention by the Italian mathematician Luca Pacioli of double-entry bookkeeping in the early 1490s. This allowed bankers to keep easy records of their profits and losses.

TOWNS AND WEALTH

Europe's wealth was concentrated in growing towns and cities. Many towns were governed by councils of citizens rather than by aristocratic rulers. The councils encouraged trade by creating markets. They set up facilities such as workshops to attract craftsmen. Residents of the town paid taxes, which went toward paying for roads and public buildings. The councils commissioned leading architects and artists to design or decorate these buildings.

▶ In the thirteenth and fourteenth centuries, European towns such as York, England, became wealthy. Many people moved from the countryside to towns to find work.

THE RENAISSANCE

SOURCE EXPLORED

The Dutch artist Johannes Vermeer painted the town of Delft in the Netherlands around 1660–1661. His view looks across the Lange Geer canal toward the town. Merchants stand beside a barge in the left foreground of the painting. The system of canals in the Netherlands made it easy to transport goods by water, and towns such as Delft had grown rich during the Renaissance. From the sixteenth century, the city produced blue-and-white pottery, known as Delftware. Other Dutch cities grew wealthy from trade with East Asia, particularly the trade in spices from the Spice Islands of what is now Indonesia.

AS THEY SAW IT

" The city of Bruges ... is well peopled, with fine houses and streets, which are all inhabited by work people, very beautiful churches and monasteries, and excellent inns. It is very strictly governed, both in respect of justice as in other matters. "

—Spanish traveler Pero Tafur describes Bruges in Flanders (Belgium) in the late 1430s.

◀ Johannes Vermeer painted three views of his hometown of Delft. Other Dutch artists also recorded the growing prosperity of the Low Countries by painting towns such as Amsterdam and Bruges.

25

Primary Sources in World History

ARCHITECTURE

As Florence grew, its citizens commissioned buildings that reflected their status. A style of building emerged based on classical architecture. Renaissance architects used classical pillars and arches. To achieve balanced proportions, they used the Greek and Roman idea of the "golden ratio." This meant they based their designs on a rectangle that was 1.62 times as long as it was wide. The architectural principles pioneered in Florence spread throughout Italy and Europe.

▼ The facade of the church of Santa Maria Novella in Florence was designed by Leon Battista Alberti in 1470. Alberti used classical proportions and details to create a harmonious whole.

THE RENAISSANCE

◀ This modern photograph of the cathedral in Florence shows Brunelleschi's dome (right) and the campanile, or bell tower, at left.

SOURCE EXPLORED

Construction began on Florence's duomo, or cathedral, in 1296. This building was designed in a medieval style known as Gothic. Gothic churches had large windows, pointed arches, tall steeples or towers, and ornately carved facades. Construction of the duomo took over 140 years. Work slowed down for 30 years after the death of the original architect in 1310, before the guild of wool merchants took over the project in the 1330s. They commissioned the artist Giotto di Bondone to design the campanile, or bell tower. In 1418 the architect Filippo Brunelleschi won a competition to design a central dome with the largest diameter of any dome in the world. The dome was completed and the cathedral was finally consecrated in 1436. The building is one of the earliest and most influential examples of Renaissance architecture.

IMPOSSIBLE DOME

Filippo Brunelleschi's revolutionary design was one of the masterpieces of Renaissance engineering. At the time, no one understood how to build such a broad-based dome across a span of 137 feet (42 m). Many architects saw the task as being impossible. Brunelleschi had to work out the method for himself. The eight sides of the egg-shaped dome are joined by eight strengthened ribs on the outside. The ribs help support the great weight of the four million bricks in the dome. The sides of the dome help to hold each other up, rather than all the weight pressing down on the walls of the cathedral below.

Primary Sources in World History

RENAISSANCE VENICE

▲ The Grand Canal is the chief waterway of Venice. The city was built on more than one hundred islands in the thirteenth century.

By 1400 maritime trade had made Venice the richest city-state in Europe. Its merchants traded throughout the Mediterranean and with the Byzantine Empire and Asia. Its wealth was reflected in its lavish architecture. Venice was governed as a republic with an elected leader, known as the doge, who came from one of the ruling families. Each year Venice marked its reliance on maritime trade in a ceremony in which the doge "married" the sea. Venetian prosperity eventually began to decline in the 1500s when the Portuguese became rivals for the eastern spice trade.

THE RENAISSANCE

◀ Titian's Frari Altarpiece is huge. It is over 20 feet (6 m) tall. The unusual perspective was intentional. The painting was designed to be viewed from directly beneath it.

AS THEY SAW IT

" The people of Venice neither have any foothold on the mainland nor can they cultivate the earth. They are compelled to import everything they need by sea. It's through trade that they have accumulated such great wealth. "

—Byzantine historian Laonicus Chalcocondyles (c. 1423-1490).

SOURCE EXPLORED

Titian (Tiziano Vecelli) was the most important artist of the late Venetian Renaissance. He made his reputation with the Frari Altarpiece painted for the city's Santa Maria Gloriosa dei Frari church between 1516 and 1518. The bold use of color and realistic style shocked the church friars, who considered having the painting removed from the church. Venice's artistic style developed separately from that of other Italian cities. Early Renaissance artists in Venice were influenced by the styles of the Byzantine Empire, with which Venice had close links. Early Venetian masters such as Giorgione and Bellini had passed on their ideas to later painters such as Titian, Tintoretto, and Veronese.

POLITICS AND GOVERNMENT

During the Middle Ages, much of Europe had been divided into small states, particularly in what are Italy, Spain, and Germany. How each state was governed depended on its individual ruler. By the start of the sixteenth century, however, strong rulers had created larger nation-states in England, France, and Spain. In Italy, Germany, and northern Europe, the many states were split between the influence of the Pope, the head of the Catholic Church, and the Holy Roman Emperor, who controlled much of Germany and northern Europe.

◄ The artist Pisanello painted this portrait of Leonello d'Este in about 1444. At the time, Leonello was the Marquis of the city of Ferrara and Duke of Modena and Reggio Emilia. He was well known for supporting artists and scholars.

THE RENAISSANCE

Aeneas Silvius Piccolomini was Bishop of Siena in the fifteenth century. Here he explains how power changes hands in the city:

> Now Siena is considered next to Florence the chief city of Tuscany; it rules many flourishing towns and possesses a wide territory. At first the nobles were in power, but when they were divided among themselves and voluntarily withdrew, the government passed to the people.... some were more able than others and as one party after another became powerful, it seized the government.

SOURCE EXPLORED

The main contribution to political thought during the Renaissance came from the writer Niccolò Machiavelli. Machiavelli was an official in the republic of Florence from 1498 to 1512. When the Medici family seized power in the city, Machiavelli was arrested and exiled. While in exile he wrote his famous book *The Prince* (1513) to explain his political ideas. Machiavelli argued that a ruler must do whatever was necessary to benefit most of his subjects. A ruler should be as harsh as required to keep order and should lie if necessary. The ends justified the means. Today such a belief is still described as "Machiavellian."

◀ *This statue of Renaissance thinker Niccolò Machiavelli comes from the facade of the Uffizi Gallery in Florence, Italy. It was carved by Lorenzo Bartolini in the first half of the nineteenth century.*

THE CATHOLIC CHURCH

The Catholic Church, led by the Pope in Rome, was the most powerful institution in Europe at the start of the Renaissance. This began to change, however, when some Europeans began to feel that it had become too worldly. In 1517 a German priest named Martin Luther began a process known as the Reformation. A new form of Christianity developed, known as Protestantism. In return the Catholic Church underwent a process of reform. It became less worldly and more spiritual.

◀ This painting shows the Italian monk Saint Francis of Assisi. In the early thirteenth century Saint Francis formed the Franciscan order of monks to try to return to a more spiritual form of Catholicism.

THE RENAISSANCE

◀ The front of Canterbury Cathedral. The cathedral houses the tomb of the twelfth-century Saint Thomas Becket. The tomb was a popular destination for pilgrims.

SOURCE EXPLORED

Canterbury Cathedral is the oldest church still in use in England. The original church dates from 597 CE and has been rebuilt numerous times. During the Middle Ages, it was a popular destination for pilgrims. During the Renaissance, the cathedral became a symbol of the rejection of the Catholic Church. In 1531 England's king, Henry VIII, left the church after the pope refused to grant him a divorce. Henry created a new Protestant church known as the Church of England or the Anglican Church. The cathedral is the seat of the Archbishop of Canterbury, head of the worldwide Anglican Church.

AS THEY SAW IT

" Papal indulgences for the building of St. Peter's are circulating under your most distinguished name ... I grieve over the wholly false impressions which the people have conceived from them; to wit—the unhappy souls believe that if they have purchased letters of indulgence they are sure of their salvation. "

—The German monk Martin Luther complains to the archbishop of Mainz about the sale of indulgences, or documents that earned their purchasers salvation after death.

Primary Sources in World History

THE PAPACY

As head of the Catholic Church, the pope was the spiritual leader of Europe's Christians. During the Renaissance he was also leader of the city-state of Rome. His involvement in worldly affairs led people to question his spiritual authority. People criticized his cardinals for having lavish lifestyles and fathering children despite taking vows of poverty and chastity. For a time in the late fourteenth century, two rival popes reigned. People wondered how the pope could now claim to be God's representative on earth.

▼ *Pope Paul III asked the artist Michelangelo to paint* The Last Judgment *on the wall of the Sistine Chapel in the Vatican. The fresco was painted between 1536 and 1541.*

THE RENAISSANCE

> During the 1400s some churchmen tried to halt the corruption of the church. Here, **Pope Pius II** rebukes one of his cardinals, Rodrigo Borgia, for his poor behavior. Borgia later became **Pope Alexander VI**:
>
> " Our displeasure is beyond words, for your conduct has brought the holy state and office into disgrace; the people will say they make us rich and great, not that we may live a blameless life, but that we may have means to gratify our passions. This is the reason the princes and the powers despise us and the laity [non-priests] mock us; this is why our own mode of living is thrown in our face when we reprove others. "

SOURCE EXPLORED

Raphael painted this portrait of Pope Leo X in about 1517. Leo was born into the powerful Medici family. He wanted to rebuild St. Peter's Basilica in Rome. He decided to raise money by selling indulgences. These certificates excused their purchasers from their sins. A German monk named Martin Luther objected that this was a misuse of church power. In 1517 he called for reform of the church. His protests eventually led to the formation of the new Protestant Church.

▲ Leo X became pope in 1513. He borrowed heavily so he could live in luxury and also so he could employ artists such as Michelangelo.

HUMANISM

The humanist philosophy of the Renaissance was based on the teachings of ancient Greek and Roman thinkers such as Aristotle, Plato, and Cicero. The name humanism reflects the importance the philosophy placed on the individual and his or her experiences, rather than the church teachings that dominated the Middle Ages. Humanism was developed as a way of understanding the world by Italian thinkers such as the fourteenth-century poet Petrarch. In the fifteenth century humanism spread throughout Europe. Some of its greatest scholars appeared in northern Europe in the sixteenth century.

◀ Hans Holbein the Younger painted this portrait of Sir Thomas More, the leading British humanist, in 1527. More's famous book *Utopia* (1516) described an ideal society based on humanist principles.

THE RENAISSANCE

▼ *This portrait is one of three that Hans Holbein painted of the Dutch scholar Erasmus of Rotterdam.*

SOURCE EXPLORED

Hans Holbein the Younger painted this portrait of the Dutch scholar Erasmus in 1523. Erasmus was famous throughout Europe as the leading supporter of humanism. Like Holbein, he spent part of his career in England. In total Holbein painted three portraits of Erasmus. The scholar gave them to his admirers, in the same way photographs are used today. In the portrait Erasmus places his hands on a book with Greek and Latin inscriptions that read "The Herculean Labors of Erasmus of Rotterdam."

In this letter from March 1501, Erasmus describes the value to humanist thinking of studying the works of ancient Greek writers:

> " I have already tasted of Greek literature in the past, but merely … sipped at it; however, having lately gone a little deeper into it, I perceive … that Latin learning, rich as it is, is defective and incomplete without Greek; for we have but a few streams and muddy puddles, whilst they have pure springs and rivers of rolling gold. I see that it is utter madness even to touch the branch of theology which deals chiefly with the mysteries unless one is provided with the equipment of Greek… "

NORTHERN RENAISSANCE

The ideas of the Renaissance reached northern Europe from the early fifteenth century. Trade had made the cities of Germany, Flanders (in present-day Belgium), and the Netherlands wealthy. New ideas spread there, particularly after the invention of the printing press in around 1440. Italian artists inspired other European artists such as Albrecht Dürer and Pieter Bruegel the Elder. Many artists traveled to Italy to study Italian art for themselves.

◀ This engraving of the Madonna and Child was created by the German artist Albrecht Dürer in 1514.

THE RENAISSANCE

In the late 1430s the Spanish nobleman, Pero Tafur, traveled through northern Europe. Here he records his admiration for Bruges in Flanders in the late 1430s:

> " It is well peopled, with fine houses and streets, which are all inhabited by work people, very beautiful churches and monasteries, and excellent inns. It is very strictly governed, both in respect of justice as in other matters. Goods are brought there from England, Germany, Brabant, Holland, Zeeland, Burgundy, Picardy, and the greater part of France, and it appears to be the port for all these countries ... "

◀ *Hunters in the Snow* was one of a series of six paintings by Bruegel showing different times of the year.

SOURCE EXPLORED

The Flemish artist Pieter Bruegel the Elder painted *Hunters in the Snow* in 1565. It shows men and their dogs returning to their village after a hunting trip. Unlike many Italian artists of the time, painters of the Northern Renaissance often depicted ordinary people in everyday settings. Bruegel specialized in scenes of peasant life. Bruegel's depiction of the Flemish landscape has a realistic foreground, with a waterwheel and people skating. In the background rise imaginary mountain peaks.

Primary Sources in World History

TUDOR ENGLAND

▲ Tudor England grew rich on trade, particularly in wool. Prosperous merchants built fine homes with timber frames and white-painted wattle-and-daub walls.

Renaissance ideas reached England during the Tudor dynasty, which began in 1485. King Henry VIII, who ruled from 1509 to 1547, was the first English king to be educated in humanist ideas. He wrote poetry and composed music. In England, dramatic changes occurred with the effects of the Renaissance and Henry's decision to break with the Catholic Church so he could divorce his wife in 1531. He began the Anglican Church, and placed himself at the head of that church.

THE RENAISSANCE

SOURCE EXPLORED

The Ambassadors is one of the most famous paintings of the Renaissance. It was painted in London in 1533 by the German artist Hans Holbein. The painting shows two important European visitors in London. The painting depicts the two men with symbolic objects such as a globe showing the heavens. Some of the objects, such as the lute with a broken string and a book of Protestant hymns, may be symbols of the religious tensions between Catholicism and Protestantism. On the floor, Holbein has painted a distorted skull. This is a variation of a popular device known as a *memento mori*, which reminded viewers of the inevitability of death.

AS THEY SAW IT

" As it was Sunday we did not go out much, and did not notice the great splendor of the dresses, because the English show themselves very well dressed every day, having splendid silken stuffs, such as we always found in Italy. Nothing is too expensive for them, and the ladies especially. "

—Philip Julius, a German nobleman, records his observations of English life in 1602.

◀ *The Ambassadors includes numerous objects representing aspects of the Renaissance. They include a portable sundial on the upper shelf and a terrestrial globe on the lower shelf.*

THE SACK OF ROME

▲ *Johannes Lingelbach painted the mutinous troops of Charles V with their loot amid the ruins of Rome in 1527.*

The late Renaissance was overshadowed by warfare. France, Spain, and the Holy Roman Empire all fought in Italy to assert their dominance. In 1527 Pope Clement VII went to war with the Holy Roman Emperor, Charles V. When Charles's troops were not paid, they decided to seize loot from Rome. On May 6, 1527, some 12,000 German troops attacked the city of Rome. They burned houses, churches, and monasteries. Clement VII was imprisoned for six months and the capital of the Catholic Church was left in ruins.

THE RENAISSANCE

SOURCE EXPLORED

This portrait of Charles V was painted by the Flemish artist Anthony van Dyck in about 1620. It was influenced by a similar portrait of Charles painted a century earlier by the artist Titian, who had worked for Charles. In 1516 Charles inherited all of the Spanish and Austrian territories of his Hapsburg dynasty, which included Spanish America. From 1519, Charles was also Holy Roman emperor. Despite being Catholic, this brought him into conflict with the papacy over political control in Italy. It was during Charles's wars with the Italian states and France that his troops sacked Rome in 1527. The painting is in the Uffizi Gallery in Florence, Italy.

▲ Van Dyck's portrait shows Charles V at the height of his power. The emperor later became weary of politics. He handed the Holy Roman Empire to his brother, Ferdinand, in 1554 and retired.

AS THEY SAW IT

" You cannot grow to early manhood merely by imagining and wishing; you must gain the knowledge and judgment which will enable you to do a man's work ... Remember how many lands you will be called upon to govern, how far apart they are, how many different languages they speak, how necessary it will be for you to know them all so that you may understand and be understood by your subjects ... "

—In 1543, Charles V decided to make his son, Philip, ruler in Spain and wrote a letter offering his advice.

Primary Sources in World History

TIMELINE

1348	The Black Death reaches Europe from Asia. Over the next three years it will kill up to a third of the population.
1378	The Western Schism begins when two men claim to be the pope, one in Avignon in France, the other in Rome.
1397	Giovanni Medici founds a family bank in Florence.
ca. 1420	Filippo Brunelleschi devises the rules of liner perspective.
1432	Jan Van Eyck completes the Ghent Altarpiece in what is now Belgium; the work is a masterpiece of the Northern Renaissance.
1434	Cosimo de Medici becomes ruler of Florence, beginning some three hundred years of Medici dominance of the city.
1435	Leon Battista Alberti writes *On Painting,* one of the key theoretical works of Renaissance art.
1436	Filippo Brunelleschi completes the dome of the cathedral in Florence.
1444	Federico da Montefeltro becomes ruler of Urbino.
1453	The Ottoman Turks overthrow Constantinople and with it the Byzantine Empire.
1455	The German printer Johannes Gutenberg uses his recently invented printing press to print a Bible.
1469	Lorenzo de Medici becomes ruler of Florence; he is noted as a patron of the arts.
1484	Sandro Botticelli paints *The Birth of Venus,* introducing mythological subjects to Renaissance painting.
1485	After the Battle of Bosworth, Henry VII comes to the throne of England, beginning the Tudor dynasty.
1492	Sailing on behalf of the Spanish crown, the Italian seafarer Christopher Columbus crosses the Atlantic to reach "the New World" of the Americas.
1490s	Luca Pacioli invents double-entry bookkeeping.
1498	Leonardo da Vinci completes *The Last Supper* on the wall of a monastery in Milan.
1507	Leonardo da Vinci begins dissecting bodies as part of his anatomical studies.

THE RENAISSANCE

1509	*King Henry VIII comes to the throne in England.*
1512	*Raphael completes* The School of Athens, *a celebrated depiction of the philosophers of ancient Greece and Rome.*
1513	*Florentine noble and state official Niccolò Machiavelli writes* The Prince, *a thesis about how rulers should best rule their subjects.* *Leo X becomes pope. He will become notorious for his heavy spending, financed by the sale of indulgences.*
1516	*The Dutch humanist scholar Erasmus publishes a Latin translation of the New Testament.* *The British humanist Sir Thomas More writes* Utopia, *an influential depiction of a perfect society.*
1517	*The German monk Martin Luther posts his objections to the Catholic Church on the door of a cathedral in Wittenberg. His action eventually leads to the Reformation and the beginning of the Protestant church.*
1519	*The Hapsburg ruler Charles V is crowned Holy Roman Emperor.*
1527	*During a war between the Holy Roman Empire and an alliance of Italian states and the French ruling dynasty, troops of Emperor Charles V sack Rome.*
1531	*King Henry VIII founds the Anglican church after the pope refuses to grant him a divorce from his first wife.*
1541	*Michelangelo completes the* Last Judgment, *a huge fresco on the wall of the Sistine Chapel in the Vatican.*
1555	*Charles V abdicates from the thrones of the Holy Roman Empire and the Hapsburg lands.*

GLOSSARY

anatomy The study of the bodies of living things and how they work.

baptistery The part of a church where people are baptized.

city-states Independent states formed by cities and their territory.

chastity Refraining from sexual relations and thoughts.

classical Relating to the ancient civilizations of Greece or Rome.

dissected Cut up a body for the purposes of medical research.

double-entry bookkeeping A method of accounting in which each transaction is entered twice, as a credit and a debit.

fresco A painting made directly onto wet, or "fresh," plaster before it dries.

hereditary Describes something passed down through generations of a family.

humanist Someone who follows the ideas of humanism, which considers secular or earthly matters to be more important than divine matters.

indulgences Certificates that excuse the purchasers from having to suffer for their sins after death.

interest A sum of money paid in return for the use of a financial loan.

linear perspective A type of perspective that uses mathematical rules leading to an imaginary vanishing point to decide the size and position of objects.

mercenary A professional soldier who fights for money rather than from loyalty to a cause.

nation-states Geographical areas that govern themselves in a way resembling modern countries.

patronage Support given by wealthy people and institutions to artists, writers, musicians, and others.

philosophers People who think in a methodical way about profound questions about life or values.

Purgatory In Catholic teaching, a state in which sinners pay for their sins and undergo purification before they are admitted to Heaven.

republics States which are governed by representatives elected by the citizens.

spiritual Related to values and beliefs rather than to everyday life.

theology The study of religion.

usury The sin of lending money at high levels of interest.

wattle and daub A building material made from interwoven sticks covered in mud.

FURTHER INFORMATION

Books

Clayborne, Anna. *The Renaissance.* Time Travel Guides. Austin, TX: Raintree, 2008.

Huntley, Theresa. *Women in the Renaissance.* Renaissance World. New York. Crabtree Publishing Company, 2009.

Kallen, Stuart A. *Renaissance Art.* Eye on Art. Detroit: Lucent Books, 2008.

Murphy, Lauren. *Art and Culture of the Renaissance World.* Ancient Art and Cultures. New York: Rosen Publishing Group, 2010.

Romanek, Trudee. *Great Ideas of the Renaissance.* Renaissance World. New York. Crabtree Publishing Company, 2009.

Rossi, Renzo. *In Renaissance Florence with Leonardo.* Come See My City. New York: Benchmark Books, 2009.

Schuman, Michael. *The Renaissance.* People at the Center of. Woodbridge, CT: Blackbirch Marketing, 2005.

Wagner, Heather Lehr. *Machiavelli: Renaissance Political Analyst and Author.* Makers of the Middle Ages and Renaissance. Philadelphia: Chelsea House Publishing, 2005.

Websites

www.ducksters.com/history/renaissance.php
An index of Ducksters articles about different aspects of the Renaissance.

www.history.com/topics/italian-renaissance
Overview of the Renaissance on History.com with links and videos.

www.leonardoda-vinci.org/
A whole site about Leonardo da Vinci, including images of all his works.

www.mrdowling.com/704-humanism.html
A guide to humanism for kids from Mr Dowling.

Publisher's note to educators and parents: Our editors have carefully reviewed these websites to ensure that they are suitable for students. Many websites change frequently, however, and we cannot guarantee that a site's future contents will continue to meet our high standards of quality and educational value. Be advised that students should be closely supervised whenever they access the Internet.

INDEX

Alberti, Leon Battista 27
Ambassadors, The 41
anatomy 19
Anglican Church 40
architecture 24, 26–27, 28
Aristotle 6, 7, 36
art 16–17, 18–19, 38–39
As They Saw It 7, 9, 15, 21, 23, 25, 29, 33, 41, 43

banking 14, 20, 21, 22–23
Boccaccio 8, 9
Botticelli, Sandro 16
Bruegel, Pieter the Elder 38, 39
Bruges 25, 39
Brunelleschi, Filippo 15, 17, 27
Byzantine Empire 10–11, 28, 29

cathedrals 33
Catholic Church 7, 22, 30, 32–33, 34–35, 40
Charles V, Emperor 42, 43
Church of England 33
cities 24–25
city-states 12–13
Constantinople 10–11

Dante Alighieri 8, 9
Delft 25
Divine Comedy, The 8–9
Duomo, Florence 15, 27
Dürer, Albrecht 38
Dyck, Anthony van 43

England 24, 30, 33, 40–41
Erasmus 37

Flanders 25, 38, 39
Florence 9, 12, 14–15, 17, 20, 21, 22, 26–27, 31
France 30

Francesca, Piero della 13
Francis of Assisi, Saint 32
Fugger, Jacob 23

Ghiberti, Lorenzo 14
Giotto di Bondone 16, 27
government 30–31
Greece, ancient 4, 6, 7, 13, 16, 26, 36

Hagia Sophia 11
Henry VIII, King of England 33, 40
Holbein, Hans the Younger 36, 37, 41
Holy Roman Empire 42, 43
humanism 36–37, 40

Istanbul *see* Constantinople
Italy 12–13, 14–15, 20, 21, 26–27, 28–29, 31

languages, European 8
Leo X, Pope 35
Leonardo da Vinci 18–19
letters of credit 23
Luther, Martin 32, 33, 35

Machiavelli, Niccolò 31
Medici family 14–15, 18, 22
Michelangelo 34
Mona Lisa 18, 19
money 21
More, Sir Thomas 36

nation-states 30
Netherlands 25, 38
Northern Renaissance 38–39

Ottoman Empire 10–11, 20, 21

Pacioli, Luca 23
painting 16–17
papacy 30, 32-33, 34–35
Paul III, Pope 34
perspective 17
Petrarch 6, 8, 36
philosophy 6, 7, 36–37
Plato 6, 7, 36
politics 30-31
Prince, The 31
printing press 6, 38
Protestantism 32, 33, 35, 40

Raphael 7, 35
Reformation 32
Renaissance, meaning 6
Rome, ancient 4, 6, 7, 13, 16, 26, 36
Rome 32, 34, 42–43

scholarship 36–37
Sforza family 18
Siena 31
Spain 30
spice trade 25, 28

textiles 20
Titian 29, 43
towns 12, 13, 24–25
trade 14, 15, 20-21, 22–23, 24, 25, 28, 29, 38
Tudors 40

Uccello, Paolo 17
Urbino 13
usury 22

Venice 20, 23, 28–29
Vermeer, Johannes 25
Virgil 8, 9

warfare 42–43